True Love

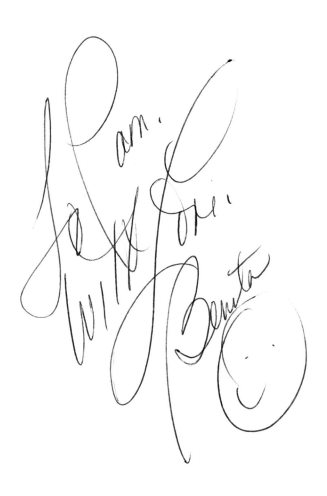

True Love

Benita E. J. Smith

All scripture has been taken from the New King James Version except where noted.

ISBN-13: 9781519147264
ISBN-10: 1519147260
Library of Congress Control Number: 2016904098
CreateSpace Independent Publishing Platform
North Charleston, South Carolina

Dedication

Thank you, Chianne, my beautiful daughter, for your years of understanding. As I was learning to be your mom, each day involved trial and error. You never questioned me but loved me unconditionally.

Your beauty radiates from the inside out, and I have learned so much from you.

I thank God for trusting me with you.

I love you dearly!

—Mommy

Contents

Acknowledgments

§

FATHER GOD, THANK YOU so much for being a Father to the father-less. Thank you for loving the good, the bad, and the ugly parts of me. Thank you for righting my wrongs.

Thank you for your kindness and patience toward me. Thank you for seeing me as the apple of your eye.

Mom, thank you so much for your unconditional love toward me. Your love and support are greatly appreciated. You are a gift from God.

To Damien, my baby brother: Thank you for your love and support. Thank you for loving me just as I am.

To Pastor John Jenkins Sr. and First Lady Trina Jenkins: Thank you for your authentic love for God. Thank you for being a visible example of humility, integrity, and excellence for the body of Christ.

Thank you, my sisters and brothers in Christ, for your labor of love toward me. It was not in vain. Thank you for the time and resources that you invested in me. I am forever grateful to God for allowing our paths to cross.

Introduction

§

TRUE LOVE IS SOMETHING THAT every human being desires to experience, but what is true love? What does it look like?

Please take a journey with me as I introduce you to my "True Love"!

It is the most beautiful experience. This type of love makes me smile. This type of love keeps me up all night. This type of love takes my appetite away. I have joy, and I am not sure why. Sometimes I am unsure why I am smiling, but I cannot stop. Not all circumstances and things around me are the greatest, but because of my true love, I am not fazed.

True love is beyond words or comprehension. I cannot explain it, but I know it when I see it and experience it.

This love fills the deep, empty places in me, and it is beyond anything that I have ever experienced.

I can fully trust this type of love. There is no fear in true love. There are no boundaries in this love.

This love does what is best for me. It may not be the most popular response at the time, but because it is true love, it is acceptable.

My True Love gave us His only begotten Son, Jesus Christ. True love caused Jesus to endure all that He endured. Jesus's true love for the Father and the world is why He laid His life down.

We are reminded of this in the Word of God. As you read and meditate on Isaiah 53, you will realize that only true love would cause someone to go through what Jesus went through. It was all for the sake of love!

Who has believed our report?
And to whom has the arm of the Lord been revealed?
For He shall grow up before Him as a tender plant,
And as a root out of dry ground.
He has no form or comeliness;
And when we see Him,
There is no beauty that we should desire Him.
He is despised and rejected by men,
A Man of sorrows and acquainted with grief.
And we hid, as it were, our faces from Him;
He was despised, and we did not esteem Him.
Surely He has borne our griefs
And carried our sorrows;
Yet we esteemed Him stricken,
Smitten by God, and afflicted.
But He was wounded for our transgressions,
He was bruised for our iniquities;
The chastisement for our peace was upon Him,
And by His stripes we are healed.
All we like sheep have gone astray;
We have turned, every one, to his own way;
And the Lord has laid on Him the iniquity of us all.
He was oppressed and He was afflicted,
Yet He opened not His mouth;
He was led as a lamb to the slaughter,
And as a sheep before its shearers is silent,

So He opened not His mouth.
He was taken from prison and from judgment,
And who will declare His generation?
For He was cut off from the land of the living;
For the transgressions of My people He was stricken.
And they made His grave with the wicked—
But with the rich at His death,
Because He had done no violence,
Nor was any deceit in His mouth.
Yet it pleased the Lord to bruise Him;
He has put Him to grief.
When You make His soul an offering for sin,
He shall see His seed, He shall prolong His days,
And the pleasure of the Lord shall prosper in His hand.
He shall see the labor of His soul, and be satisfied.
By His knowledge My righteous Servant shall justify many,
For He shall bear their iniquities.
Therefore I will divide Him a portion with the great,
And He shall divide the spoil with the strong,
Because He poured out His soul unto death,
And He was numbered with the transgressors,
And He bore the sin of many,
And made intercession for the transgressors.

—*Isaiah 53:1–12*

It has taken me many years to recognize my True Love. This is the love of my Father, God in Heaven.

I have searched and searched, looking for love in *all* the wrong places.

The love that I share with God is beyond words and comprehension. True love goes beyond the good, the bad, and the ugly. It is unconditional. It lovingly walked with me as I went down many wrong roads and finally changed course, and my True Love was still there.

This true love says no and closes doors that should not be opened. I could not understand why some relationships and people were removed from my life, but it was all for love. My True Love did this in my best interests.

I think of this like parenting. As my daughter grew up, sometimes I had to tell her no. I wanted her to be happy, but I truly loved her and wanted the very best for her.

This is the same situation with my Father in Heaven. Because of His true love for me, for many years He said no, not yet, or wait. I finally understood that it was all due to His love for me.

As I look back over my years, I can see God's true love for me in every area of my life.

With my acceptance of this true love, I experienced *truth and freedom*!

I can see, experience, and trust God's love—the truth about me and the relationships that are and will be in my life, the freedom to love others just as they are, the freedom to love and accept myself, and the freedom to love, worship and praise God freely!

The true love that God has demonstrated to me has been evident in so many areas of my life. I want to share them with you.

This journey has not been easy, but I would not trade it for the world. I am so thankful to have had the opportunity to experience and recognize this true love. I want the world to know about this unexplainable, undeniable, and indescribable love.

It is said that if you observe how things in nature live, you will see a close resemblance to how we live our lives. The butterfly has captured my attention, and I will share with you why. The butterfly is one of the most fascinating insects. There are over twenty-eight thousand different types of moth and butterfly species worldwide.

The humble beginnings of a butterfly give way to a complete life-cycle. Butterflies are considered an advanced insect because they go through four separate stages in their lives. These four stages are completely separate from one another, and each has a significant purpose in the life of the butterfly.

Please stick with me; I am going somewhere here!

The first stage of the butterfly is the egg. The female butterfly can lay between a few hundred to thousands of eggs. The eggs are layered on leaves and twigs. If the temperature is right, the embryo inside the egg can develop into a caterpillar in one to three weeks.

Stage two is the caterpillar. The embryo has now developed into a caterpillar and eats its way out of the egg. The caterpillar will eat leaves and plants as it grows. This is the feeding-and-growth stage. As the caterpillar grows, it sheds its skin. This can happen four or more times as the body rapidly grows.

Stage three is the pupa phase. The caterpillar will travel long distances in search of an ideal place to pupate. The caterpillar rests, and the metamorphosis takes place. Metamorphosis is the changing of physical form, [1]defined as a marked change in appearance, character, condition, or function.

The caterpillar transitions into an adult in this stage. Internal changes occur. This is a nonfeeding stage with no movement. A cocoon (a hardened case) forms around the caterpillar. From the outside, it looks as if there is no physical activity in the cocoon. Temperature will dictate how long the caterpillar is in this stage. It can take a few weeks or several months.

Stage four is the butterfly. A beautiful butterfly emerges from the cocoon. It usually has very large wings and many beautiful colors for us to enjoy.

---

1 (The American Heritage College Dictionary Third Edition, 1993)

This is why I am so fascinated with the butterfly.

As I travel through life with the Lord, I reflect on the years in which nothing seemed to be going on in my life. However, in the quiet places, inner work was being done on my character and my inner self.

On the outside, nothing appeared to be happening, but in this place, God was molding and shaping my character.

As I look back, every stage of my life has had a purpose, and each stage had its own part to play on this journey.

The beauty of the butterfly reflects the glory of God. As we come out of our cocoons and shed our old selves, God receives the glory that we endured, and we are transformed into the image of His Son, our Savior Jesus Christ.

The story of a butterfly's transitions is beautiful. This is how our lives are. They are simply beautiful. As we transform, our beauty is shown to the world, and we are all different—different colors, different shapes. We are at different stages in our lives and ages. This beauty is captivating.

So I ask you to walk through this journey with me.

I will share with you the different stages of my life, and hopefully you will see and understand my cocoon, caterpillar, pupa, and butterfly experiences. By the end of this book, I pray that you are able to enjoy the beautiful colors that God has blessed me with through His true love for me and for you.

This book was written out of love for God and for His people. It is my desire that all will know the outrageous love that God has for them.

May this book inspire and minister to the length, width, and breadth of our Father's love. This is not just for me but also for all of His creation to experience.

May this book share the true love of God.

Thank you for responding to me;
you've truly become my salvation!
The stone the masons discarded as flawed
is now the capstone!
This is God's work.
We rub our eyes—we can hardly believe it!
This is the very day God acted—
let's celebrate and be festive!
Salvation now, God. Salvation now!
Oh yes, God—a free and full life!

—*Psalm 118:21–25, The Message*

CHAPTER 1

A Daughter

§

Every good gift and every perfect gift is from above,
and comes down from the Father of lights, with whom
there is no variation or shadow of turning.

—*James 1:17*

MY MOTHER HAS DEMONSTRATED THE unconditional love of God to me. As I sit and reflect on my life, the one consistent thing that I see is my mother demonstrating this love to me. God blessed me with my mother. She loves me—when I'm at my best or when I'm at my worst. I have made so many bad decisions and gone down many wrong paths, but my mother has never said "I told you so" to me. She has always quietly supported me in every stage of my life.

Journaling is so therapeutic for me, and I can recall a journal entry that I wrote about my mother on February 18, 1997. It reads:

I must say that I have a great mom. She has always given me the opportunity to make my life's mistakes and to find the answers later if necessary. She has always respected my opinions. This is a plus in my eyes. It is so important to have respect for one another. I have had talks with my friends and some of them do not give their mothers a chance to talk about things with them; they already figure that their parents would not understand their problems. My mom has even been there for my friends in desperate situations. It is so funny how you can take your parents for granted. It is an easy thing to do. I just do not know what I would do if something happened to my mother. She is both a mother and friend to me. She helps me out with my daughter. She is a great listener, never judgmental; that means a lot to me. Lord knows, I have made some dumb decisions. I feel very lucky, and I know that having an understanding mother makes life so much easier. My dad has always been a little softer than my mom. He cannot handle too much. If something bad is going on in the family, he will be so upset that he will stop talking. He gets so nervous and sometimes has had to get off the phone. My mom can handle a lot. Things may bother her, but she lets you know what you need to know and when you need to know it. I am very fortunate to have her.

God has truly demonstrated His love toward me by blessing me with my mother.

As true love, God knows what you need without you saying it.

My mother's love and support are beyond words. I truly cannot comprehend how God in His infinite wisdom knew exactly the type of mom that I would need. He is loving, and even though you do not see it all the time, He is so patient and waits until you can gain a better understanding of the very gifts that He has blessed you with. Sometimes you can totally miss that these gifts are right there before your eyes.

Growing up, I was consumed by my own hurts and emotional pains, low self-esteem, anger, and unforgiveness. These things overwhelmed me and for some time caused me not to appreciate what I had right in front of me: the tangible true love of the Father on this earth, in the form of my mother. The love of a mother is unconditional, and she is God's incarnate way of demonstrating His love for me.

I got it! I recognize the true love of my Father because God blessed me with my mother. True love is also demonstrated when I am able to be a daughter to my mother, who contains so much love. I am beyond grateful.

This love is a true blessing from above. The true love of the Father is demonstrated on earth through a mother who quietly supports and loves her daughter.

I pray to God that as a daughter, I love and have loved my mother as I should love her. I pray that as a daughter, I give my very best to my mother. I pray that I take every advantage to demonstrate my gratefulness to her for the true love of my Father and to show gratitude for this love. I pray that as a daughter, I demonstrate this same true love to my mother, because truly she is a gift from above!

It took me so many years in my role as a daughter to get this thing right. As a young woman growing into adulthood, I did not fully understand my role. It is a privilege and an honor to be a daughter. It took me some time to realize that my mind had to be renewed to fully understand the blessing of being a daughter. The true love of the Father allowed me to be a daughter and to have the mother that I have. I am so grateful to God that my mind was renewed and that I had a chance to see from His perspective what it means to be a daughter.

God has truly blessed me with a mother who truly loves me. I have no doubts about this and do not question this love.

I pray to God that I never, ever take the true love of my mother for granted. May I always recognize that it is an honor to be the daughter of Shirley A. Jones, who is God's physical representative of His true love for me.

Amen.

And above all things have fervent love for one another, for "love will cover a multitude of sins."

—1 Peter 4:8

CHAPTER 2

A Youth

So I will restore to you the years that the
swarming locust has eaten,
The crawling locust,
The consuming locust,
And the chewing locust,
My great army which I sent among you.
You shall eat in plenty and be satisfied,
And praise the name of the Lord your God,
Who has dealt wondrously with you;
And My people shall never be put to shame.
Then you shall know that I am in the midst of Israel:
I am the Lord your God
And there is no other.
My people shall never be put to shame.

—*Joel 2:25–27*

MY PARENTS WERE VERY YOUNG when they got married. We moved to Washington, DC, in 1968, when I was three years old. I was an only child for a very long time. I was very timid as a child, more than likely because I spent a great deal of time alone. I was afraid of everything. As a little girl in elementary school, I always found myself alone. I never quite fit in with any crowds. I was bullied and teased. I could never figure this out. Why did the kids not want to be my friend? As I grew up, my self-esteem decreased more and more. This caused me to examine myself and wonder what was so wrong with me. I wanted to be shorter. I was much heavier than the other kids were, so I wanted to be smaller than I was. My hair was short, so I wanted longer hair. My feet were skinny and narrow, so I wanted smaller feet.

I look back at this time and recognize how it contributed to feeling bad about myself later in life. I grew up ashamed and embarrassed by my life and by how I looked.

In addition to me feeling ashamed and embarrassed by my life and how I looked, I also felt shame and disappointment over my family life.

My dad was very sad, and he chose to drink because of the pain that he felt internally. He loved his family—and I knew that he loved me dearly—but the truth of the matter is that my dad was hurt by things that he had experienced as a young man; he was never able to resolve these issues, and this caused him to drink his troubles away.

So imagine my dad's drinking was embarrassing, and on top of that, I was embarrassed about how I was created and looked.

This is a very bad combination!

The enemy of my soul had me right where he wanted me to be: beaten down and oppressed.

All through elementary school and into junior high, I did not connect with other kids. I just never fit in!

As I moved into high school, things got a little better. I became involved in activities at the school, which helped a little. However, there was still something not quite right. Quietly, I still struggled with low self-esteem and with not fitting in. My family issues had not gotten any better. My mom and dad separated when I turned eighteen years old, and everything looked so dark. When my dad left, it greatly impacted my life. I did not know how much until years later.

By the time I graduated from high school, I was completely clueless. I did not know whether to go into the service or just work; I was oblivious to how important college would be and how it would benefit me in the long run. I decided to just work.

This time of my life was difficult for me. Nothing good was happening, and I was just sad about how my life had turned out. Life went on, and my sadness was never addressed. I began to make error after error. I was falling deeper into depression, losing more self-esteem, and developing a hardness of heart.

At nineteen, I decided to move out of my mom's home. This was crazy! I had an apartment and was working, but I wasn't making any real progress in life—just going through the motions!

When I reflect on this time, I can see how my life spiraled out of control. The enemy was able to work on me at a very young age. Unless you recognize his strategy, it can cause you to travel down the wrong paths.

I can now see this strategy clearly. I have been able to acknowledge where I was and discern what lessons I learned in the process.

First, I learned that I needed to know that God loved me and that I was "fearfully and wonderfully made" (Ps. 139:14). Everything that God creates is beautiful because it is forged in His image. He created my physical appearance, and it was marvelous in His eyes. Nothing was missing from me, and nothing was broken, but I needed to know this. No, I would not fit in, because I was never supposed to conform to this world. God never wanted me to fit in.

Fear leads to doubt, and this leads to a lack of faith. Both of these left me defeated in life.

I met a young man in high school, and our families became acquainted. He was my first boyfriend. His family took me to church, and at sixteen years of age, I gave my life to Christ.

I didn't realize how significant this was, but I knew that something inside of me was drawing me toward God. I see that as a little girl, the presence of God was always with me. I remember having to ride the Metrobus to school by myself; it scared me silly, but God would always have people strategically in place to help me. I gravitated toward some older women, and I would talk with them. I think about having to walk to school and the bus stop and being so afraid, but God was always there.

I do believe that I met my boyfriend's family so that they could lead me to church, where I could be drawn to God. God waited patiently for me through my younger years. He loved me through my mess and waited for me to accept myself!

I recognize now that my relationship with my earthly father played a huge part in my life and influenced how I dealt with relationships and life itself.

My dad loved me; I know this. He did not quite know how to demonstrate this love, and he was not able to speak words of encouragement to build me up.

My relationship with my dad was vital to me as a young person, and I now recognize how much a young lady needs a strong and healthy relationship with her earthly father. This is essential; it will contribute to healthy self-esteem, emotional health, and healthy relationships with others, especially those of the opposite sex. I understand now that this was an important part of my life. I hungered and thirsted for something, but I had no idea what it was. I did know that I was searching. I began to search for love in all the wrong places!

My dad and I were able to maintain our relationship even though he drank. I loved my dad, and I know that he knew it. Unfortunately, my dad had many health challenges, and he passed away. I thank God for restoring our relationship and allowing my dad to know that I loved him despite what he was going through and what our family had gone through.

I thank God that He is a Father to the fatherless.

God has given me the time to reflect on and to recognize my mistakes, but He also comforted me through the lessons I learned.

My heart has been healed, and I love myself just as God created me. When I look at myself, I no longer want to change anything that God gave me.

I thank God because in retrospect, I know that He was with me the entire time. Even before giving my life to Him, I could see that He was there. During those hard childhood years, I can see that He blessed me with unconditional love for my dad and the ability to see and know that in spite of my dad's troubles, he loved me.

I thank God for recovering all the years that were stolen from me. I thank God for healing my heart. There is no bitterness. He has removed the shame of my youth. I am no longer ashamed of how I grew up.

Those things made me stronger and wiser. I understand now that I could not fit in, and I am so glad that I did not.

God is truly the lifter of my head and the best friend and companion that I could ever have. Being rejected by my peers drove me into His loving arms.

I learned not to despise my small beginnings. God has made everything beautiful in its time.

He has made everything beautiful in its time. Also He has put eternity in their hearts, except that no one can find out the work that God does from beginning to end.

—Ecclesiastes 3:11

CHAPTER 3

A Woman

§

For You formed my inward parts;
You covered me in my mother's womb.
I will praise You, for I am fearfully and wonderfully made;
Marvelous are Your works,
And that my soul knows very well.
My frame was not hidden from You,
When I was made in secret,
And skillfully wrought in the lowest parts of the earth.
Your eyes saw my substance, being yet unformed.
And in Your book they all were written,
The days fashioned for me,
When as yet there were none of them.

—PSALM *139:13–16*

I CAN REMEMBER NOT LIKING anything about myself when I was a little girl. Because of the way I was created, I saw so many things that I would change if I could. My hair was not long or thick enough; I was much heavier than all the other little girls were. My feet were long and narrow and seemed much bigger than everyone else's feet. I could go on and on. I did not like what I saw when I looked in the mirror.

9

I grew up with these unhealthy thoughts. As I got older, I would see other women and wish that I looked like them or could be them. Even my height was an issue. Oh, I wished that I were really short—not taking into consideration that my weight would be an even greater issue if I were shorter.

Imagine growing up, you look at yourself every single day and not fully enjoy or embrace who you are. I felt this way for many, many years.

I would have an internal conversation of what it would be like if I looked differently. The sad part about this is that no one would ever know.

You see, you can fix up the outer person, but the inside can still be broken and messed up. This described me! Clothes became a big factor, as did hairstyles and the like. The Bible clearly addresses this issue:

> *Do not let your adornment be merely outward—arranging the hair, wearing gold, or putting on fine apparel—rather let it be the hidden person of the heart, with the incorruptible beauty of a gentle and quiet spirit, which is very precious in the sight of God.*
>
> *—1 Peter 3:3–4*

I had no idea that everything I needed physically, I already possessed.

Things did not change for me until I fully encouraged and embraced the true love of God.

This love was there all along, but I could not see it. My eyes were blind to this great love. God loved me so much that He created a unique woman: me!

Wow! I see things beautifully now that I have fully accepted and embraced the true love of my Heavenly Father.

I now recognize the inside and outside beauty of Benita.

This beautiful love of God has allowed me to accept how God creatively formed and fashioned gifts, skills, and talents and so strategically placed them inside of me.

Please let me share a little with you about Benita.

My Love Languages:
Quality time

Acts of service

If someone wants to communicate his or her love and appreciation to me, it is best shown through these primary love languages.

My Spiritual Gifts:
Motivational: Mercy
My heart compels me to remove others' stress and to share their burdens. I have a heart of compassion toward others, and I like to demonstrate this by giving hugs and by being there for them through rough times. I will walk through the valley with you.

Ministry: Help
My goal is to assist the people in leadership positions in any way needed. I also look to help the needy.

Manifestation: Discernment
God has truly blessed me with the ability to recognize what is of God verses what is of the world. This discernment allows me to see if matters are of the flesh or of the devil.

God created me with the Spirit-Controlled Temperament of "Melancholy." All of the temperaments have strengths and weaknesses. Guess what. Benita has had to accept and embrace both sides! Moses also had this temperament. Melancholy is the richest of the temperaments.

My Strengths:

* Gifted
* Analytical
* Perfectionist
* Self-disciplined
* Industrious
* Self-sacrificing
* Aesthetic (appreciate beauty or good taste)
* Creative
* Loyal/faithful

My Weaknesses:

* Moody
* Deeply emotional
* Easily offended
* Pessimistic
* Negative
* Critical and picky
* Theoretical
* Impractical
* Suspicious
* Vengeful
* Self-centered
* Indecisive

Please understand that I shared this not to boast or to complain. I did not share my weaknesses to feel sorry for myself. This is to acknowledge that I fully embrace the workmanship of God. He makes no mistakes, and I accept His Sovereign work and decision on how He formed and fashioned me.

Some additional things that I have found out about myself:

- Organized
- Good with time management
- Encouraging
- Disciplined
- Loyal
- Committed
- Trustworthy
- Family oriented
- A life coach
- Dependable
- Motivating
- Compassionate
- Supportive
- Genuine
- Very sensitive

God is purposeful and strategic beyond our understanding, and His ways are so above ours. He is masterful in all that He does. He formed and fashioned us, and His skill in doing so is incomprehensible.

Did you know that about 99 percent of our DNA is the same as everyone else's, leaving only 1 percent that makes us unique? Can you imagine this? There is only a small difference between you and me, which should cause us to never be envious or jealous of one another, and we should celebrate the uniqueness in one another.

Thanks be to my God that I am in a totally different place now! God's true love has caused me to embrace who I am and how I was created by Him.

I like myself, and I like and enjoy everything about me. I thank God for creating me as a woman. I enjoy what I see in the mirror. I know that God created me, and He makes no mistakes. I know that He loves me just as I am, with or without makeup.

He loves me, and He loves you. God's love is true for us no matter what!

Yes, I must do the things that are required to take care of this physical body, such as work out, and take care of my skin, teeth, and hair. However, I keep it all in the proper perspective so that it does not define who I am; these things are simply enhancers.

I recognize that I represent God as I am physically in this world. I was created in the image of God.

Beloved sisters in Christ, women of God, celebrate your beauty inside and out! It is marvelous in our eyes!

This was the Lord's doing;
It is marvelous in our eyes.

—*Psalm 118:23*

CHAPTER 4

A Wife and A Single

§

*And don't be wishing you were someplace else or with someone
else. Where you are right now is God's place for you. Live and
obey and love and believe right there. God, not your marital
status, defines your life. Don't think I'm being harder on you
than on the others. I give this same counsel in all the churches.*

—*1 Corinthians 7:17, The Message*

I WAS TWENTY-ONE YEARS OLD and married. Wow, how in the world
did I get there? Everything moved fast.

By the time I was eighteen years old, my dad had moved out of
the home, and my life had taken a downward spiral for sure! I began
to look for love in all the wrong places. I was hurt and confused, and
I did not know it. I already had many low-self-esteem issues. I was in
a very low place inside and nobody knew it.

I was working in the banking industry in the heart of downtown
Washington, DC, where I met my soon-to-be husband, Anthony.
Both of us were very young. We became acquainted and began talking, and before we knew it, we were headed down a serious road. He
was nineteen years old, and I was twenty-one at the time that we got

married, so as you can imagine, we really had no clue what we were about to get ourselves into.

We had no idea that marriage was for grown folks!

Before we knew it, we were married. We enjoyed one another, and at times I found myself running home because I was so excited to see him. We did everything together.

We did not have a lot of money, but we never went hungry.

After a year of marriage, we talked about having children. A child would add to our family. We still had no clue of the huge responsibility that we had toward one another and to the life of another—a child. After three years of marriage, we found ourselves expecting a baby.

We both were young and naïve. But God's true love for us stepped in and graced us for the journey. Throughout my entire pregnancy, Anthony was excellent. He went to every single doctor's appointment with me; he missed not one appointment. I had an excellent pregnancy, and God provided for us because, again, we had no idea what we were doing.

We worked together throughout the entire pregnancy. Anthony did his part. He worked and took care of us, and he never complained. After our daughter was born, our focus changed significantly; we found ourselves concentrating on this little person all time, and we began to neglect our marital relationship.

As a wife, I had no biblical concept of my role in and responsibilities to this marriage. This was not good for our marriage at all. As happened, it caused an invisible barrier to form between Anthony and me. We communicated less and less.

It was unfortunate that six years into the marriage and with our daughter only four, we found ourselves separated and then divorced.

As I look back over this time, I can see my many, many mistakes.

We needed so much help, and we needed godly wisdom. God had provided us with many people in our lives to assist us, but we were not mature enough to seek their guidance and council. I now know that we needed to be spiritually connected with God and with one another. Without this connection, it is much harder to survive, if you survive at all.

I found myself so hurt and disappointed. I was a wife, and I knew that I wanted to be a wife. However, I had no sense of value in being a wife and didn't know how to be one.

The failure of my marriage was added to the pain I already had. Let's just say that I was a real mess on the inside!

In 1998, my mother, daughter, and I became members of the First Baptist Church of Glenarden (FBCG). When we began attending church, Sunday after Sunday for one year I would come into the building, sit down in the sanctuary and cry. I would just cry. Not baby tears—big tears! I was so hurt.

The FBCG has so many classes and workshops geared to the family. In my quest to get answers for my life, I began to take these classes. The more biblical teachings I was exposed to, the more I was able to recognize my responsibility in my marriage as well as why it failed.

This made me cry even more.

One day I was sitting in church, and the spirit of God clearly spoke to me. I could finally be honest with myself and say, "Benita, you would be married if it was not for you!" I finally came to terms with the truth. I could take full responsibility for how I had handled Anthony and our marriage, and it was not good.

This made me cry even more!

I began to study more of God's Word and His heart concerning divorce and family. I soon recognized the importance of family and the role of a wife in the marriage.

God blessed me by putting me in the company of godly women—women who were excellent wives. The importance of a wife and her significance to her family and husband became clear to me.

After much breaking on the inside, studying, and godly counseling, I knew many years later that I had to right my wrong. After being discipled in many women's groups and sitting at the feet of powerful teachers, my heart had been softened, and I now could go back to Anthony to seek reconciliation.

I went to people whom God had placed in my life for accountability. They shared their support and told me that it was the right thing to do. My final test to assure myself that it was the right thing to do was to ask my Pastor, John K. Jenkins Sr.

In 2007 I shared my situation with Pastor Jenkins and told him what was in my heart to do. He gave me clear instructions to go to the bookstore and get the book *The Rebuilder's Guide*, by Bill Gothard: Institute in Basic Life Principles. Pastor Jenkins would not allow me to make excuses but instructed me to do what was right by seeking reconciliation with Anthony.

I cried because I did not want to do this, but I had to be obedient to God and to the authority that He had placed over me.

Anthony and I had finally become friends through it all. We were getting along really well. At the time, he was living in another state, but he was traveling to Maryland to bring our daughter back home from visiting with him for the summer.

This was the perfect time. After much accountability and support, it was now time to do this—to seek reconciliation.

The week prior to us talking, I cried a lot. In my mind, I saw Anthony accepting the proposal for reconciliation. Why not? He and I were not together anymore, but we were getting along great.

I just cried. I was dealing with so many issues, knowing that I had to humble myself and seek reconciliation out of obedience to God and to my accountability partners.

On the evening before our meeting, a beautiful sister from FBCG sat in the car in the church parking lot with me and allowed me to cry and cry about what I had to do. She did not judge, but encouraged me and quietly sat there with me as I went through my many emotions. She prayed with me and quietly gave me her love and support.

Anthony did come into town, and I shared with him all that I had learned. I admitted my failures in the marriage, taking full responsibility, and he listened respectfully. I shared with him that I had spoken with Pastor Jenkins. I asked him if we could reconcile the marriage, and I apologized for not being the wife that I should have been to him.

He listened, and then he politely told me that if this had been years ago, he might have accepted. However, at this time, he could not accept. He told me to go back to Pastor Jenkins and tell the pastor that he had said no. Now, he said this not in an arrogant way but in the way of order. It was as if a huge weight was lifted from us both after we had this discussion. He now has a great deal of respect for our relationship and for Pastor Jenkins.

As I look back on the marriage, I can clearly see that you must be prepared for the role of a wife. It is not something that you can jump into or play with. I could say it is a higher calling. God has given the role of a wife huge influence within her home. It is a major responsibility, but it is a blessing to have the opportunity to be a wife.

I would definitely say preparation is needed, such as studying the Word of God, learning what God says about the role a wife should play and how she should conduct herself. I now know that your dedication and love for God will make you an excellent wife. God has clearly laid out the roles and responsibilities of a wife, and it is to a woman's advantage to study this prior to getting married.

God blessed me by healing my heart. I know that He has forgiven me, and I have forgiven myself for this failed marriage.

I pray to have the opportunity to be married again. Being a wife is a beautiful and rewarding role. With much prayer and honor to

God, a woman can be an exceptional wife and called by her husband a good and perfect gift from above.

The story does not end with Anthony and me. A year or two later, he did remarry and moved back to the area. I had the opportunity to become acquainted with his wife. I tell you, you never know what this journey will bring you. We all would talk from time to time, so much so that his wife would call me to ask me things. Are you serious? Yes, I am so serious!

One day I asked her if her two sons could attend church with us and they both agreed that it was OK. They were young adults, but they did not drive at the time.

This is the funny part: I drove over to their home, and I picked them up. I waved at Anthony and his new, beautiful wife. I was still single! What was this about? I couldn't do anything but laugh. I was having an out-of-body experience!

Guess what. Both of her sons gave their lives to Christ at the FBCG! Hallelujah!

Two souls were won for the Kingdom.

This is bigger than our little minds can even imagine. God was blessing us all, and I knew then that this was not about me for sure.

God gets the glory in this story!

Today, Anthony and I have a better relationship than before. I know without a doubt that I can go to him for help. He will be there for me, and I am there to help him. We can talk, and we still can come together on behalf of our daughter.

God has healed my heart. He has renewed my mind regarding the role of a wife in a marriage from a biblical perspective and not the world's perspective. I have a better understanding of the family structure and the role of the wife. If God allows me the opportunity to marry again, I would take it as an honor. It is a privilege to be a wife.

God truly blessed me throughout this situation. I am forever grateful for His mercy and grace as I walk through this journey of love, forgiveness, healing, and restoration.

I have worked through my past, and I now have found myself single and saved.

This journey is much different. There was so much pain after the divorce, but God already had a plan and people in place to assist me in getting back on His perfect path of truth and freedom. God loves me that much.

God does *all* things well, and as I was transitioning, He began wooing me back to Him. I recognized His true love on this journey as a single woman once again!

You never know who or what God will use to draw you closer to Him. In my case, he used a complete stranger.

I would often see a gentleman at our agency's gym. We would not speak, but his face became familiar to me. One day I was in a college course outside of work, and this same gentleman was there. We recognized one another, acknowledged that we were coworkers, and began to talk. As I reflect on that meeting now, I am 100 percent sure that this man, Marvin Beard, could see right through me.

I was so broken. I felt like a failure after the divorce. I was done so to speak. Marvin began to share with me and gently asked me thought-provoking questions. One profound question he asked me was how was my relationship with God was. I was so out of it at the time. I could not see the relationship between the two. What did what I was going through have to do with what church I attended and my relationship with God?

Well, I knew for sure by then, and Marvin knew, that I was his assignment. We began to talk more as I shared my situation with him. He politely listened and never judged me with his words or his eyes. For some reason, I felt comfortable with him, and I shared and I shared. One day, Marvin suggested having lunch together because he would like to share some things with me. I was so broken, and I did not hesitate to accept this invitation. I had been looking for love in all the wrong places, and I needed as much help as I could possibly get.

Marvin and I walked to a place for lunch near the office one day. We sat down, and he shared the Good News of the Gospel of Jesus Christ with me. God's love was shining brightly through Marvin, and I opened my heart to Jesus through Marvin right there in the middle of a restaurant. Right there in the middle of lunch hour in a restaurant, I rededicated my life to Christ. My heart was being redirected back into the hands where it had always belonged: those of Jesus Christ.

As Marvin and I walked back to the office, he said, "Benita, your life will never be the same." This was so true. Marvin purchased a study Bible and a Bible concordance for me. He began to share with me as God was sharing with him.

I relate this testimony because this was part of my healing process as a newly single woman of God in the Kingdom. God allowed this encounter because the pieces of my life were so broken. God used a godly man, Marvin Beard, to assist Him in getting me back on the road of restoration and healing.

I so thank God for Marvin Beard and the time that he took to share with me.

God is the lifter of my head, and His outrageous true love for me was apparent in this predestined encounter with Marvin.

Through this relationship with Marvin, my mind-set about men was renewed. This is a man of God—a man who desired to have a relationship with me without ulterior motives. Marvin desired to pour in and not take away. Marvin shared his views from a godly perspective of how a woman of God should carry herself. He also shared with me that my skirts at the time were too short. He pulled me to the side and gently encouraged me to pay attention to the lengths of my dresses and my deportment. Wow, I needed to hear this. I did not want to attract the wrong type of people to my life, but first I had to change me from the inside out. Marvin always shared without judgment. This was all new to me. It was now my goal to live saved, single, and blessed for God.

My revelation included the fact that sex outside of marriage is a sin. God was working it out. Marvin and I talked about the institution of marriage and also about how now was the time to allow God to keep me as a single woman.

How timely it was to have this man of God in my life. This was nothing but God's true love for me. I thank God for Marvin; he journeyed with me without judgment but with love. I really needed this relationship of love. God used him in a mighty way, and I am so happy that God blessed Marvin with a beautiful wife, Dorothy.

Marvin, please know that your labor of love was not in vain!

As I said, this journey as a single has been a tremendous blessing.

In 2000 I made an adamant decision to live a life dedicated to God as a single woman. This journey has its ups and downs, but God is a keeper. I trust and believe in preparation. I have the benefit of continually learning who I am in Christ. When I got married, I was broken, in debt, and just a mess. God has been teaching me through the years. I had the opportunity to learn the importance of financial freedom and to learn about my temperament, my love language, and most importantly, God's true love for me.

Brethren, if a man is overtaken in any trespass, you who are spiritual restore such a one in a spirit of gentleness, considering yourself lest you also be tempted.

—Galatians 6:1

CHAPTER 5

A Parent

§

Train up a child in the way he should go,
And when he is old he will not depart from it.

—*Proverbs 22:6*

AT THE AGE OF TWENTY-SIX, I was married, and I had prayed to God
and asked Him for a beautiful baby girl to be born around my birthday.
God does grant you the desires of your heart. On September 17, 1991,
I gave birth to a beautiful baby girl, Chianne. What a blessing she was
to her dad and me. We had no idea what we had gotten ourselves into!
I remember being at the hospital and the nurse bringing Chianne into
the room for me to feed her. My response, as I just sat there and looked
at this small being wrapped in a blanket, was, "I do not know how to
feed her." I was so unsure of my abilities as a mom. Thank God for His
help, love, and mercy. Parenting is the most serious job that anyone can
ever have! Being a mother has been a true learning experience.

I became a single parent by divorce when Chianne was four years
old. This totally changed the dynamics of being a parent. Although
her father and I had separated, he never separated himself from
Chianne. We both made some huge sacrifices to ensure that she was
prepared for life.

I certainly see why God instructed marriage first and then raising children second. Of course, I know that it does not always turn
out like that; ideally, it is to the parents' advantage to raise the children together. This is how big of a job it is.

Raising my daughter has been a blessing. I have learned many lessons—some harder than others. In raising a child, you have to learn
patience just as he or she is learning to be more patient with you.

We laugh now at some of our intense moments. My daughter has
been a significant person on this journey of mine.

At the age of five, Chianne looked at me one day and asked,
"Why don't I go to church?" At that time, my mind was totally somewhere else. Still, I took her question to heart, and that was when my
mom and I began our quest to find a church. We thought we were
doing it just to satisfy the child, never knowing that God had used
a child to demonstrate His true love toward us. We began visiting
churches, and someone recommended the First Baptist Church of
Glenarden, located in Landover, Maryland. The visiting of other
churches was over—we had found our church home!

In January 1998, Pastor John K. Jenkins Sr. was preaching on
the scripture Jeremiah 29:11, "For I know the thoughts that I think
toward you, says the LORD, thoughts of peace and not of evil, to
give you a future and a hope." Chianne and I took that walk up to
the front of the church, as I wanted to rededicate my life to Christ.
Chianne looked up at me and said, "Mommy, why are we up here?"
Little did Chianne know that God had used her to save our lives. I
had been headed to hell quickly, and she was used to snatch my feet
out of the miry clay.

Chianne and I have had some very hard days. The financial
struggles were very difficult. There were long days at school, and
Chianne was very active in school. Thank God that He gave us
the strength to endure. It was not only that I had patience but

also that Chianne demonstrated a tremendous amount of patience with me. Many days I did not have enough money to do the things that she desired, but she never complained, even during the years she and I had to share a bedroom. Yes, you read that correctly. A mother and daughter had to share a room, and there was no space to divide us. We had to look at one another all day and night. It hurt me, and I spent many days crying and stressing myself out because I wanted things to change. Through it all, I lost sight of the good that would come of this and I did not know how this would create a bond between us. This, too, we are able to laugh about now.

Chianne has been a true treasure to have in our lives. She has a beautiful spirit, and God truly blessed her with the strength to endure. She has been with me through some very significant points on this journey of life!

In December 2000, Chianne and I drove to check on my dad, and unfortunately, we discovered that my dad had passed away at his home. I had called my dad several times the night before. He was not responding to my phone calls, so Chianne and I drove to his home. I will never forget how God used Chianne when she was nine years old during this dark moment in life. As the security guard opened the door, Chianne and I stood there with her arms wrapped around my waist tightly. The security guard looked at me as she radioed in to someone that there was an unconscious male on the floor. She then looked at me and shook her head without saying a word. I knew exactly what that meant. My dad had passed away. When she looked at me with a very sad look, my knees buckled. Chianne tightly held onto me, never letting me go. She never opened her mouth to ask me any questions. She remained quiet as I began to cry and while I conducted business in my dad's resident-business office.

As I reflect on this, it makes me cry all over again. God had placed this baby there to support me, and she did. God had used her again to help me through a difficult time.

The other significant time Chianne was used in my life was one day when we were driving home from her gymnastics practice. It was a beautiful evening; the sun was still up, and we were discussing if Chianne wanted to stop at McDonald's for dinner. As we were driving, a little boy rode off a hill on a bicycle. He slammed into the front of my car, hitting his bike on top of my car and hitting his head on my windshield, shattering the glass. He fell to the street, screaming. I stopped the car; I was in shock, and I could not move. I was just sitting there in complete shock, but Chianne got out of the passenger seat, checked on the little boy, returned to the car, opened the car door, and yelled, "Mommy, you have to get out of the car!" Chianne proceeded to walk back to the little boy to check out the scene, and then she came back to the car to tell me what was going on.

It was a blessing that the little boy had no broken bones. There was no blood, and he was doing just fine! Another blessing was that there were so many witnesses, including a plainclothes police officer, who saw the little boy cross in front of the car.

Again, Chianne was used by God during a significant incident in my life!

I shared this because as I think back over my life, I recognize that during this time in my life, a great deal of growth took place.

Raising Chianne caused a holding pattern in my life that God used. God had given me a focal point: raising this little girl the way God would have me do. No relationships and no dating—just concentrating on being the best mom that I could be. Many days and nights were spent sitting in the parking lot waiting for Chianne to come out of school from after-school activities, but I would not change a thing! I thank God for allowing me to be a mother. I have learned so much, and I have had to humble myself by going back to Chianne and apologizing to her for my words and my actions.

Parenting is a very humbling experience, and God has graced us to get through it.

It has not been easy, but I would not change a thing. I am beyond grateful for the opportunity to raise Chianne.

Chianne is now twenty-four years old; she is currently living in Atlanta, Georgia, in graduate school for social work. This was a huge adjustment for us both. She had been my focus for many, many years, but now it was time for her to fly. Even in her decision to relocate, God was teaching me that both of our seasons had now changed. It was time for Chianne to utilize all that she had learned and to begin her own journey with God. We now both have to trust God even more for one another and continue our journeys on our own.

God has been so gracious and kind to us. I thank God more than words can express for trusting me to be Chianne's mother.

Every good gift and every perfect gift is from above, and comes down from the Father of lights, with whom there is no variation or shadow of turning.

—James 1:17

CHAPTER 6

A Sister in Christ

§

Behold, how good and how pleasant it is
For brethren to dwell together in unity!

—PSALM 133:1

As A LITTLE GIRL, I always wanted a sister. God blessed me with a brother who is eleven years younger than I am. Growing up, I truly missed not having a sister.

Only God knows how you feel and what your heart desires.

Just as God had orchestrated my footsteps leading me to be a part of the First Baptist Church of Glenarden (FBCG) ministry, He had already put things in place for me to experience the love of sisterhood.

The journey began in 2003 at the FBCG Ministry Center. God had blessed me with the opportunity to be mentored one whole year with five other beautiful women of God by a reverend at the church. The reverend would meet with us every Friday night in the basement of her home. No fanfare, no eating and playing—we dived into the Word of God, and we were challenged to apply and obey the Word that we were reading and studying.

The reverend was obedient to God. Once the time had come for us to leave the group and apply what we had learned, she released us with the challenge to be about our Father's business. We completed this year full of anticipation for what God would do next.

I personally was not quite sure what to do. I was just allowing God to dictate my footsteps, and I was watching Him open doors that I did not ask for or anticipate would open for me.

One day, my mom and I were sitting in church before the service, and a minister from the church shared that it had been laid on her heart to develop a small group study for women, a group that would meet in their homes. I was very grateful that she shared this with me, and I was beyond grateful for the opportunity to be a part of the study group.

The group studied from a four-part *"MasterLife* series of books" by Avery T. Willis Jr. The goal of this study was to develop men's and women's ability to make Christ the Master and center of their lives. It is a challenging series of books, as you learn to memorize scripture and to journal on a daily basis.

This was totally out of my comfort zone. I did not know any of the women in the group very well. All that I knew was that God had opened this door and I was going to do this even if I was afraid!

Well, in I went! We started out meeting at the minister's home, and eventually we met at different homes of the ladies within the group.

I had no idea what this journey would bring, but nevertheless, I was going to do this.

As we dove into the books, each book was doing its work on the inside of us. We dealt with our personalities. As we were getting to know one another, we had to learn to be very transparent. Now, remember, I did not grow up with sisters, so this was all new to me. Only God knows how very challenging that was. I was dealing with low self-esteem, and I was very insecure as a person.

Because of God's true love for me, it was now time to deal with these issues. These were matters of the heart—things that I had hidden from others and even from myself. I had trouble in the beginning

with opening up because I felt out of place. I was not a college graduate; I was a divorced woman working in a non-professional position
in the administrative field. This, to me, was not good at all!

The ladies had better educational backgrounds and were in professional fields—professors, doctors, and the like.

As you can see, I had issues. But God! As this journey proceeded,
God soon allowed me to address my issues, and I was soon able to
share this with the ladies. This time was God's gift to me.

It took about nine months to walk us through things in the
MasterLife series of books. It was a true blessing, and we became
very close. God blessed us with love for one another through the
positive and negative things we have experienced. Only God knew
the result. It was laid on the minister's heart to allow other women
to experience this which birthed a whole new ministry at the church.

Each of the original five members recommended other women
to the group and shared their experiences in it, and the numbers
increased and increased. We would rotate and meet at the homes
of the women who were in the group. The women were eager, and
because of the changes in the women who had gone through the
MasterLife books, the numbers continued to grow. Then other
churches became aware of this life-changing experience for women
through the series of *MasterLife* books.

I personally experienced a life-changing time in my life. As we
bonded through prayer and giving to one another, I learned what
true sisterhood is all about, and God blessed me with sisters. Sisters
for life!

I learned to rely on my sisters. As storms came upon our lives, we
went through them together.

In 2005 a young lady in our original group called me to go to
lunch with her for my birthday. She met me at work for lunch, and
out of the blue, she said that God had laid it on her heart to give me

her car. Now mind you, my car was giving me problems and would eventually break down completely during this time. When she and I met for lunch, I could tell that God had clearly spoken this to her heart and that it was settled within her spirit to be obedient to what He had asked her to do. I was so overwhelmed by what she had said that I told her to please give me some time to digest this. I was astonished by God and my sister!

Again, remember that I did not grow up with sisters, and it was hard to receive this kind of love. I needed time to process what was happening. This was God's true love being demonstrated through a sister.

I did accept the car. On a Saturday, my sister and I met so that she could hand over the car. Her mom accompanied her to bring the car to me. She got out of the car which was spotless, had very low mileage, and was full of gas. She gave me the manual, all needed information, and the title, as well as the information about where she took the car for service.

She gave me the keys and signed the title. My sister said goodbye, and she did not look back or discuss this transaction with anyone. My sister did not purchase another car for some time after this. My sister did this for me? God only knew how this would minister to me. I call this car jireh, as God is my Provider. This was a beyond-words experience for me.

I could go on and on. This was a life-changing experience for me. This was God's gift to me. As I did not have biological sisters, God had blessed me with sisters in the Kingdom of God—eternal sisters. I will never, ever forget this experience or forget how these sisters of God blessed my life.

We do not get a chance to see or talk with one another as much, but these sisters will always be my sisters. God's true love for me will be forever remembered through my experience with them.

Wow, God's true love! I thank God so much for His love. I thank God for blessing me abundantly, above and beyond what I could ask, think, or imagine!

Two are better than one,
Because they have a good reward for their labor.

—Ecclesiastes 4:9

CHAPTER 7

A Friend

§

A friend loves at all times,
And a brother is born for adversity.

—*Proverbs 17:17*

MY MOTHER, DAUGHTER, AND I joined the First Baptist Church of Glenarden (FBCG) in 1998. At that time, I was so broken and confused. I found myself a single parent with no clue how to raise a little girl. I desperately needed to raise her to go in a completely different direction than I had gone.

During my very first year at the FBCG, I just sat and cried the entire time. I was so hurt and disappointed about my life—the things I had done and the things that I had not done.

After some time, God raised my head, and I saw a young lady in the church who was a single mother and very actively involved in the church. Her name is Desiree James.

Desiree was following hard after Christ, and I could see it. At the time, she was overseeing the Single-Parenting Ministry. I got involved in the ministry right on time. We would have fellowships at Desiree's home, and there was plenty for our children to do also.

A few of the single parents in the Single-Parenting Ministry were also able to take a much-needed road trip to the Shenandoah Mountains Skyline. This gave us a chance to encourage one another and to have a fun time.

I quietly admired Desiree from afar. She walked as she was called. I was able to observe how she handled others, and most importantly, how she was handling me.

As a single woman of God, it was so important to me to have strong and positive accountability in my life. I did not know what to expect, but God's true love for me was evident in Him allowing our paths to cross.

As I became more actively involved in the Single-Parenting Ministry, I began to get involved in other ministries within the church too. The Singles Ministry was the next step. I took the "Single and Blessed" class, where Desiree served as the assistant to the facilitator. The Single and Blessed class totally turned my world upside down. Everything that I thought I knew about relationships was totally wrong. This class was a blessing. At the end of the class, we signed a covenant to maintain our purity until or if God blessed us and brought someone into our lives for marriage.

As the years passed, Desiree began to teach this course herself. Guess what. God blessed me and allowed me to assist her for a semester. Desiree has invited me back several times since then to sit on a panel of singles to share our stories. What accountability!

As you can see, Desiree and I have walked together for many, many years.

God has allowed me to see through His eyes the love and beauty of a friend/a sister in Christ. I am beyond grateful to God for this relationship. I wish I could say that through the years of knowing Desiree, it has all been a delightful party for me, but it has not. There have been many dark days for me, and Desiree has been standing right there through them all!

One day in particular stands out in my mind. I was going through something, and I called her from Prince George's Community College. I was walking, and I became so overwhelmed with hurt that I just sat down outside of the school and poured my heart out to Desiree over the phone. I was so discouraged with the things that were happening all around me. She quietly listened, not offering any advice but just listening. She never passed any judgments on anyone involved. She just quietly listened, and that spoke volumes for me. I will never, ever forget that day. I was so, so broken, and it was so, so dark.

I have observed that in this relationship, we have been there for one another through every spectrum of life thrown at us. The scripture tells us to rejoice with those who rejoice and to weep with those who weep. Desiree has done just that in our relationship.

When God opened many doors in my life through the years, Desiree rejoiced and encouraged me so much. Her disposition toward me has been very consistent.

I am so thankful that I recognize the gift that God has given me. Friendships are a blessing to our lives. God has loved me through her, and I am beyond grateful for this gift of friendship.

My prayer is that I am a friend to her in the same way. I pray that I am found to be loving, consistent, and faithful to our relationship!

Imitate me, just as I also imitate Christ.

—1 Corinthians 11:1

CHAPTER 8

A Worker

§

And whatever you do, do it heartily, as to the Lord and not
to men, knowing that from the Lord you will receive the
reward of the inheritance; for you serve the Lord Christ.

—COLOSSIANS 3:23–24

WHEN CHIANNE WAS BORN, I was at home with her for an entire
year. Now, mind you, God loved me so much that He took excellent
care of us. We were only living off Anthony's income, but we lacked
absolutely nothing!

I truly did not understand and appreciate the year off that I had to
spend time with my daughter. I wanted to work! I began applying for
jobs everywhere. I had worked in the banking industry and then retail.

I applied to the federal government, and one day I received a call.
This call was from out of nowhere, or so I thought.

God blessed me, and I was interviewed and hired.

It was a blessing because there were many applicants, and my
supervisor later shared with me that I was not qualified for the job.
However, for some reason he wanted to give me a chance. It took me
a minute, but I soon realized that God's true love had a plan for me
on this employment journey.

A journey it has been. This supervisor turned out to be a blessing from above. I entered the federal government with no idea of its operation. I was from the banking industry, which was very conservative. I began the journey pretty clueless and didn't know which direction to go, but I began to learn my way and to meet people. Unfortunately, I did not have a plan, and I just settled and conformed. I was now making friends, and not applying myself, but looking around trying to figure out why I had not been promoted.

God loved me so much that my supervisor began challenging me. He started giving me projects and pretty much making up assignments to motivate me. It took many years of many supervisors and other people coming and going before I could figure out why I was not progressing professionally.

My supervisor soon retired, and I was now wondering what to do next. I had done many jobs in other offices, trying to find my way. Now I must say God truly blessed me with supervisors who were very good and motivated me. The responsibility was on me. They were doing their part. However, something was missing, and it took many, many years for me to figure it out.

My Pastor, John K. Jenkins Sr. had preached many sermons on the importance of an employee's role; I should strive for excellence and work as unto the Lord. I had heard him many times, but this time I was really listening. God was speaking to my heart, and I knew some things needed to change.

I finally got it; I now began to go to work focused on serving as unto the Lord. I had developed habits that were not up to God's standards, such as socializing and not giving 100 percent of my time at work for work. Honestly speaking, I was doing everything else except spending the time working and doing the job that I had been hired to do—no, I was not. Oh, and I must add that I was still looking around trying to figure out why everyone around me was being promoted and I was not.

One example of how I changed my mind-set is when I was working and a gentleman came to our office to be interviewed for a position. It was placed on my heart to seat him in the conference room for the interview, to get him a glass of ice water, and to serve him. I did not focus on me but serving him as unto the Lord. It was now clicking for me!

I finally woke up. God's Word through Pastor Jenkins had finally penetrated my heart. Now I remind you, God's true love still allowed me to have excellent supervisors who were very tolerant and kind to me. This was nothing but God's great grace and mercy.

As I shared with you, years and years had passed, and I was finally judging myself. I was now recognizing that my character needed some maturing. This federal job was a holding pattern—a place of much maturing for me. I had some growing up to do.

I began to serve in this federal job while recognizing my assignment as a disciple and a woman of God. I began to work and to change many bad habits that I had developed over the years—no, I will not list them!

My former supervisor had retired and I now had a new supervisor. As it was a divine setup by God, he began to mentor me. This supervisor would sit down with me every two weeks to discuss my professional goals; he challenged me to return to school for my undergraduate degree and to look for jobs with promotion potential.

Let's take a break here!

God placed it on the heart of my supervisor to help me find a job that allowed for promotion. Talk about the love, mercy, and grace of God! This is it!

Back to the story: My supervisor and I would meet regularly. He was holding me accountable to register for classes and to look for job announcements.

One day we were meeting, and he gave me an announcement for an opportunity to work in the administrator's office in our agency. I looked at it and immediately made excuses in my mind as to why I could not do the job. I read the announcement repeatedly and came back to him that day not sure that I should apply. He recommended that I inquire about it and take it from there. I was obedient and thought about it. Yes, I doubted my abilities; I was comfortable where I was but also wanted to do something different and get a promotion. I wanted to move on because I had been in that office for so long. I had grown up in the office where I was, and now I knew it was time for me to fly.

I did apply for the job, and I went back to my supervisor to let him know. He explained several of the next steps I needed to take, and as I left his office, the Holy Spirit told me clearly to be obedient and to do everything that he told me to do—and I did.

I received a call for an interview that was held by a panel of people. Please keep in mind that I had not been through the interview process in years. I prayed and asked God to help me, and he did. I prayed and released the outcome to God. I was in a new place, and I submitted to God's will. I was very thankful to have been selected to be interviewed.

May I back up a little bit? My former supervisor who had retired had challenged me to create a portfolio of my work experiences and personal achievements. He told me to create one—the models have portfolios, so why shouldn't I? Guess what. One of the ministers at the First Baptist Church of Glenarden blessed me, sowed the idea of a portfolio case in my life, and walked me through creating the portfolio. I now had one with my resume, certificates, and awards.

My life was visually laid out in this portfolio, and I was now able to share it in my interviews.

God is so excellent! Even in my clueless state, He was still blessing me. What manner of love is this?

Back to the story. Please forgive me; when I think back on this, it just blows my mind.

I was called for a second interview with the executive director of our agency. Now, this was the second week. Three weeks later, I was called to interview with the administrator himself, whom I would be working for. He sat down and told me what was expected in this position and that there was no room to play.

Well, I was notified that I had been selected for the position.

Wow, God's timing was so perfect. I was beyond thankful for this job.

In December 2011, I began my new position and stepped out of my comfort zone. I was solely depending on God. The team that I joined was outstanding, and I finally began to learn the importance of teamwork, as the office was very fast paced and the team was there to provide the help that was needed to get things done.

I was overwhelmed by being in the job and learning so much. I clearly knew that I was there to serve, and the teachings of Pastor Jenkins were in my heart and mind. I was there to make sure my supervisor had everything that he needed to be successful.

A year had passed, and my new supervisor was called to serve in an acting deputy-secretary position within the agency. What do I do now, Lord? I was just getting used to working with him.

The Holy Spirit told me to begin to accept the changes and to keep my focus. No complaining. Just go with the flow. So I did. Whatever was asked of me, I did it. I even had to pack up my desk again and move to another area. The Holy Spirit said to be quiet and do not complain! Just go with the flow.

It was some six months later when I received a call from the office that my former supervisor who was now serving as the acting deputy secretary. I was offered an opportunity to be on a detail in the office that he was now serving in. A detail allows an employee to work and perform the necessary duties to maintain the flow of an office with a vacancy to fill. This detail is for a specific duration of time.

What? I quickly accepted the opportunity to work once again with my supervisor, in a new office with totally new duties and responsibilities.

I was astonished at this opportunity. While on the detail, I was told that the position that I was detailing for would be advertised and that I could apply for it. Yes, my mouth was open. I did apply and I did get the job. I recognized that God had opened a door for me. I knew that again, I was not qualified, but God's love was giving me this opportunity.

Some months later, my supervisor was officially placed into the higher position that he had been acting in.

God had promoted me twice in two years. I was speechless! God only knows that I am beyond thankful.

I now look back and realize that I had so much to learn. I needed God to mold and shape me. God needed to work some things out of me and to mold my character. I know that I still have plenty of work to do, but I am not the same person who came to the agency in 1992.

I am so grateful to God and to the men and women who took the time to pour their love into me and encourage me to strive to do better. One of my former supervisors said to me one day, "Benita, the only person who can hold you back is you." Wow! God has truly demonstrated His true love for me through these men and women who have taken the time to help me along the way.

I am enjoying my new place of employment because I am now much further from my comfort zone but much closer to God!

Not that I have already attained, or am already perfected; but I press on, that I may lay hold of that for which Christ Jesus has also laid hold of me. Brethren, I do not count myself to have apprehended; but one thing I do, forgetting those things which are behind and reaching forward to those things which are ahead, I press toward the goal for the prize of the upward call of God in Christ Jesus.

—Philippians 3:12–14

Conclusion

§

GOD'S LOVE CHANGES YOUR PERSPECTIVE on life, which allows you to better love others.

I am so thankful for this time alone with God. I wouldn't change it and can't put a price on it. My True Love has allowed so many men and women of God to cross my path and to hold me accountable, to pour God's love into me, and to provide wisdom and correction in my life—gentle correction that was firm but not judgmental.

God, thank you so much for your true love. Your love is beyond my comprehension. Your love has been outrageous toward me. I can see Your hand clearly, and I thank you for loving me. You love me with an everlasting love. Nothing can separate me from Your love.

Thank you for healing and restoring me. Thank you for keeping me and caring for me as the apple of Your eye. Thank you for correction that was not shameful. Thank you for gently leading and guiding me in all truth. Thank you for freedom. Thank you for the freedom to love.

I love You, and my heart and my affections are for You and You alone.

Thank you for loving me through others. Your love has been demonstrated through the love of others toward me.

I cannot share in this book all that You have done for me. It is beyond words. You have exceeded my expectations. Thank you forever!

I love You because You first loved me.

Father, you are my True Love!

—Benita

A new commandment I give to you, that you love one another; as I have loved you, that you also love one another. By this all will know that you are My disciples, if you have love for one another.

—John 13:34–35

Scriptures to Encourage Your Soul

Jeremiah 31:3

*The L*ORD *has appeared of old to me, saying:*
"Yes, I have loved you with an everlasting love;
Therefore with loving kindness I have drawn you."

Song of Solomon 2:4 Amplified Bible, Classic Edition

He brought me to the banqueting house, and his banner over me was love [for love waved as a protecting and comforting banner over my head when I was near him].

1 Peter 1:8-9, The Message

You never saw him, yet you love him. You still don't see him, yet you trust him—with laughter and singing. Because you kept on believing, you'll get what you're looking forward to: total salvation.

Romans 8:35–39

Who shall separate us from the love of Christ? Shall tribu-
lation, or distress, or persecution, or famine, or naked-
ness, or peril, or sword? As it is written:
"For Your sake we are killed all day long;
We are accounted as sheep for the slaughter."
Yet in all these things we are more than conquerors through Him who
loved us. For I am persuaded that neither death nor life, nor angels
nor principalities nor powers, nor things present nor things to come,
nor height nor depth, nor any other created thing, shall be able to
separate us from the love of God which is in Christ Jesus our Lord.

Psalm 32:8

I will instruct you and teach you in the way you should go;
I will guide you with My eye.

Isaiah 61:10

I will greatly rejoice in the LORD,
My soul shall be joyful in my God;
For He has clothed me with the garments of salvation,
He has covered me with the robe of righteousness,
As a bridegroom decks himself with ornaments,
And as a bride adorns herself with her jewels.

Psalm 63:7-8

Because You have been my help,
Therefore in the shadow of Your wings I will rejoice.
My soul follows close behind You;
Your right hand upholds me.

1 Peter 5:7

casting all your care upon Him, for He cares for you.

John 14:27

Peace I leave with you, My peace I give to you; not as the world gives do I give to you. Let not your heart be troubled, neither let it be afraid.

Psalm 37:4

Delight yourself also in the LORD,
And He shall give you the desires of your heart.

Zephaniah 3:17

The LORD your God in your midst,
The Mighty One, will save;
He will rejoice over you with gladness,
He will quiet you with His love,
He will rejoice over you with singing.

Exodus 33:14

And He said, "My Presence will go with you, and I will give you rest."

Philippians 4:13

I can do all things through Christ who strengthens me.

Psalm 55:17

Evening and morning and at noon
I will pray, and cry aloud,
And He shall hear my voice.

Psalm 62:5-6

My soul, wait silently for God alone,
For my expectation is from Him.
He only is my rock and my salvation;
He is my defense;
I shall not be moved.

Deuteronomy 31:6

Be strong and of good courage, do not fear nor be afraid of them; for the LORD your God, He is the One who goes with you. He will not leave you nor forsake you."

Psalm 23:1-4

The LORD is my shepherd;
I shall not want.
He makes me to lie down in green pastures;
He leads me beside the still waters.
He restores my soul;
He leads me in the paths of righteousness
For His name's sake.
Yea, though I walk through the valley of the shadow of death,
I will fear no evil;
For You are with me;
Your rod and Your staff, they comfort me.

Psalm 73:23

Nevertheless I am continually with You;
You hold me by my right hand.

Jeremiah 31:25

For I have satiated the weary soul, and I have replenished every sorrowful soul.

Jeremiah 31:13

Then shall the virgin rejoice in the dance,
And the young men and the old, together;
For I will turn their mourning to joy,
Will comfort them,
And make them rejoice rather than sorrow.

Isaiah 41:13

For I, the LORD *your God, will hold your right hand,*
Saying to you, 'Fear not, I will help you.'

Micah 7:7

*Therefore I will look to the L*ORD*;*
I will wait for the God of my salvation;
My God will hear me.

Job 8:7

Though your beginning was small,
Yet your latter end would increase abundantly.

Isaiah 32:18

My people will dwell in a peaceful habitation,
In secure dwellings, and in quiet resting places,

Isaiah 46:4

Even to your old age, I am He,
And even to gray hairs I will carry you!
I have made, and I will bear;
Even I will carry, and will deliver you

.

Luke 1:37

For with God nothing will be impossible.

Hebrews 6:10

God is not unjust; he will not forget your work and the love you have shown him as you have helped his people and continue to help them.

Psalm 94:18-19, New International Version

When I said, "My foot is slipping,"
your unfailing love, LORD, supported me.
When anxiety was great within me,
your consolation brought me joy.

John 14:14

If you ask anything in My name, I will do it.

Psalm 73:25

Whom have I in heaven but You?
And there is none upon earth that I desire besides You.

Deuteronomy 10:21

He is your praise, and He is your God, who has done for you these great and awesome things which your eyes have seen.

Psalm 100, The Message

On your feet now—applaud God!
Bring a gift of laughter,
sing yourselves into his presence.
Know this: God is God, and God, God.
He made us; we didn't make him.
We're his people, his well-tended sheep.
Enter with the password: "Thank you!"
Make yourselves at home, talking praise.
Thank him. Worship him.
For God is sheer beauty,
all-generous in love,
loyal always and ever.

Made in the USA
Columbia, SC
01 July 2017